THIS IRELAND TRAVEL JOURNAL
BELONGS TO...

NAME:________________________________

DATE OF ARRIVAL IN

IRELAND:____________________________

DATE I LEFT IRELAND WITH A HEAVY

HEART:_________________________________

Ireland Travel Journal

An illustrated diary and keepsake of your trip to Ireland

Plain Scribes Press

www.plainscribespress.com

Paperback: 978-1-960227-77-5

Hardcover: 978-1-960227-76-8

A Message to The Traveler

Dear Traveler,

As the creator of this Ireland Travel Journal, I hope that, in years to come, this journal becomes a cherished keepsake, a legacy of memories shared with family and friends, immortalizing your journey around Ireland.

Go n-éirí an bóthar leat
– *Guh nigh ree uhn boh-hur luth.*
May the road rise to meet you!

Séamus Mullarkey

I TRAVELED TO IRELAND WITH THE FOLLOWING GREAT PEOPLE

The Story of How I Came to Visit Ireland

What I'll Always Remember About Ireland

My Advice for Anyone Going to Ireland

How Ireland Changed Me

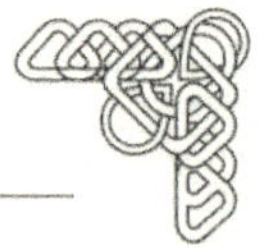

TODAY'S DATE : ______________________________

What I'll Remember Most About Today…

--Experiences – Sights – Feelings--

Daily Page

Today I Traveled From:

To:

My Accommodation Today:

Best Food or Drink Today

Things I Did Today:

Souvenirs or Presents I Bought:

Quote or Phrase of the Day

TODAY'S DATE : ______________________

What I'll Remember Most About Today…
--Experiences – Sights – Feelings--

Daily Page

Today I Traveled From: ______________________

To: ______________________

My Accommodation Today: ______________________

____

Best Food or Drink Today ______________________

____

Things I Did Today: ______________________

____

____

____

____

____

____

____

Souvenirs or Presents I Bought: ______________________

____

Quote or Phrase of the Day

____

____

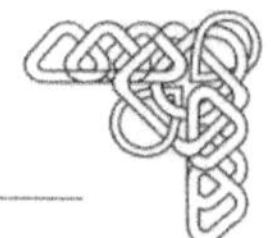

TODAY'S DATE : ______________________

What I'll Remember Most About Today…
--Experiences – Sights – Feelings--

Daily Page

Today I Traveled From: ______

To: ______

My Accommodation Today: ______

______

Best Food or Drink Today ______

______

Things I Did Today: ______

______

______

______

______

______

______

______

Souvenirs or Presents I Bought: ______

______

Quote or Phrase of the Day

______

______

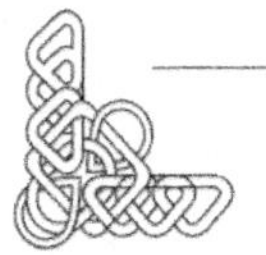

TODAY'S DATE : ______________________

What I'll Remember Most About Today…
--Experiences – Sights – Feelings--

g

Daily Page

Today I Traveled From: ________________

To: ________________

My Accommodation Today: ________________

Best Food or Drink Today ________________

Things I Did Today: ________________

Souvenirs or Presents I Bought: ________________

Quote or Phrase of the Day

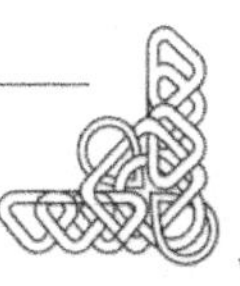

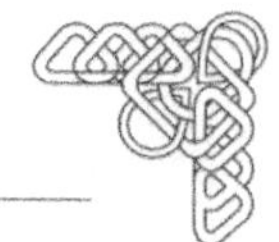

TODAY'S DATE : ______________________

What I'll Remember Most About Today…
--Experiences – Sights – Feelings--

Daily Page

Today I Traveled From: ______________________

To: ______________________

My Accommodation Today: ______________________

____

Best Food or Drink Today ______________________

____

Things I Did Today: ______________________

____

____

____

____

____

____

____

Souvenirs or Presents I Bought: ______________________

____

Quote or Phrase of the Day

____

____

TODAY'S DATE : ____________

What I'll Remember Most About Today…
--Experiences – Sights – Feelings--

Daily Page

Today I Traveled From: ______

To: ______

My Accommodation Today: ______

______

Best Food or Drink Today ______

______

Things I Did Today: ______

______

______

______

______

______

______

______

Souvenirs or Presents I Bought: ______

______

Quote or Phrase of the Day

______

______

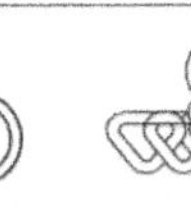

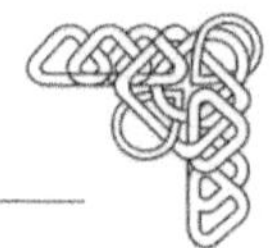

TODAY'S DATE : ______________________

What I'll Remember Most About Today…
--Experiences – Sights – Feelings--

Daily Page

Today I Traveled From: ________________

To: ________________

My Accommodation Today: ________________

Best Food or Drink Today ________________

Things I Did Today: ________________

Souvenirs or Presents I Bought: ________________

Quote or Phrase of the Day

TODAY'S DATE : ______________________

What I'll Remember Most About Today…
--Experiences – Sights – Feelings--

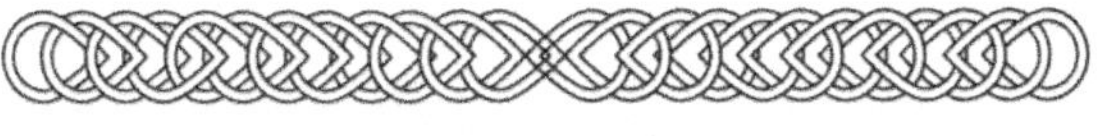

Daily Page

Today I Traveled From: ____________________

To: ____________________

My Accommodation Today: ____________________

Best Food or Drink Today ____________________

Things I Did Today: ____________________

Souvenirs or Presents I Bought: ____________________

Quote or Phrase of the Day

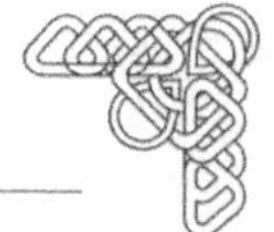

TODAY'S DATE : ______________________

What I'll Remember Most About Today…
--Experiences – Sights – Feelings--

____

____

____

____

____

____

Daily Page

Today I Traveled From: ______________________

To: ______________________

My Accommodation Today: ______________________

____

Best Food or Drink Today ______________________

____

Things I Did Today: ______________________

____

____

____

____

____

____

____

Souvenirs or Presents I Bought: ______________________

____

Quote or Phrase of the Day

____

____

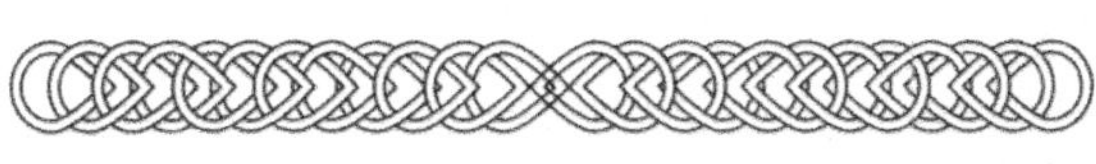

TODAY'S DATE : ______________________

What I'll Remember Most About Today…
--Experiences – Sights – Feelings--

Daily Page

Today I Traveled From:

To:

My Accommodation Today:

Best Food or Drink Today

Things I Did Today:

Souvenirs or Presents I Bought:

Quote or Phrase of the Day

TODAY'S DATE : ______________________

What I'll Remember Most About Today…

--Experiences – Sights – Feelings--

Daily Page

Today I Traveled From:

To:

My Accommodation Today:

Best Food or Drink Today

Things I Did Today:

Souvenirs or Presents I Bought:

Quote or Phrase of the Day

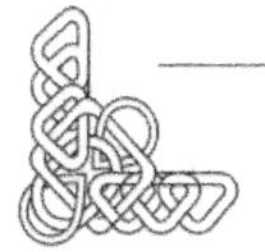

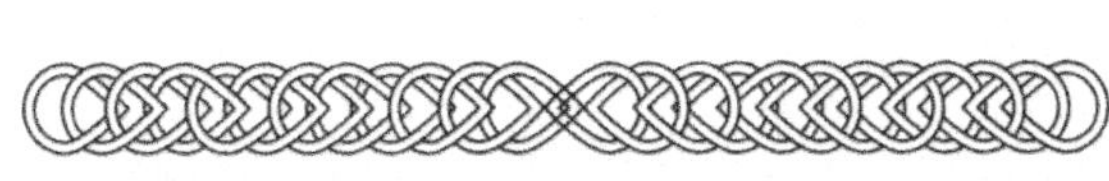

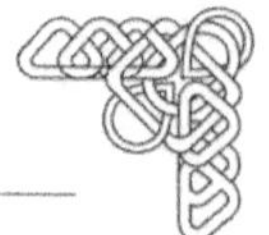

TODAY'S DATE : ______________________

What I'll Remember Most About Today…
--Experiences – Sights – Feelings--

Daily Page

Today I Traveled From: ____________________

To: ____________________________________

My Accommodation Today: ________________

Best Food or Drink Today ________________

Things I Did Today: ______________________

Souvenirs or Presents I Bought: ______________

Quote or Phrase of the Day

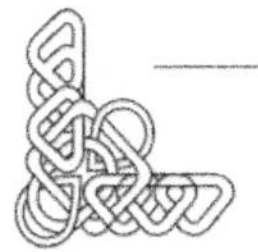  

TODAY'S DATE : ______________________

What I'll Remember Most About Today…
--Experiences – Sights – Feelings--

g

Daily Page

Today I Traveled From:

To:

My Accommodation Today:

Best Food or Drink Today

Things I Did Today:

Souvenirs or Presents I Bought:

Quote or Phrase of the Day

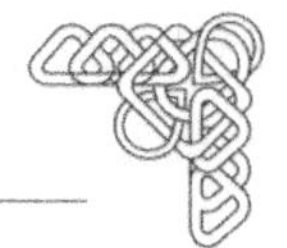

TODAY'S DATE : ______________________

What I'll Remember Most About Today…
--Experiences – Sights – Feelings--

____

____

____

____

____

____

Daily Page

Today I Traveled From: ______________________

To: ______________________

My Accommodation Today: ______________________

____

Best Food or Drink Today ______________________

____

Things I Did Today: ______________________

____

____

____

____

____

____

____

Souvenirs or Presents I Bought: ______________________

____

Quote or Phrase of the Day

____

____

TODAY'S DATE : ______________________

What I'll Remember Most About Today…
--Experiences – Sights – Feelings--

Daily Page

Today I Traveled From: ____________________

To: ____________________

My Accommodation Today: ____________________

____

Best Food or Drink Today ____________________

____

Things I Did Today: ____________________

____

____

____

____

____

____

____

Souvenirs or Presents I Bought: ____________________

____

Quote or Phrase of the Day

____

____

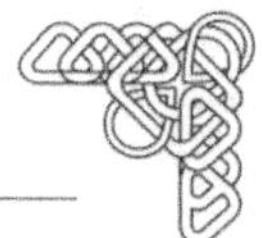

TODAY'S DATE : ______________________

What I'll Remember Most About Today…
--Experiences – Sights – Feelings--

Daily Page

Today I Traveled From: ______________________

To: ______________________

My Accommodation Today: ______________________

____

Best Food or Drink Today ______________________

____

Things I Did Today: ______________________

____

____

____

____

____

____

____

Souvenirs or Presents I Bought: ______________________

____

Quote or Phrase of the Day

____

____

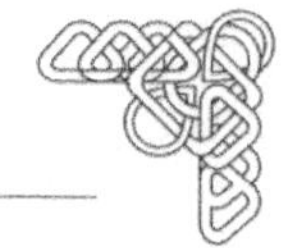

TODAY'S DATE : ______________________

What I'll Remember Most About Today…
--Experiences – Sights – Feelings--

____

____

____

____

____

____

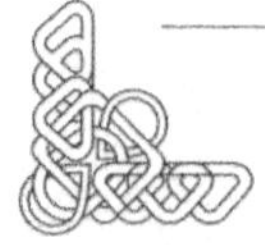

Daily Page

Today I Traveled From: ______

To: ______

My Accommodation Today: ______

______

Best Food or Drink Today ______

______

Things I Did Today: ______

______

______

______

______

______

______

______

Souvenirs or Presents I Bought: ______

______

Quote or Phrase of the Day

______

______

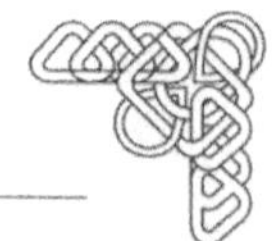

TODAY'S DATE : ______________________

What I'll Remember Most About Today…
--Experiences – Sights – Feelings--

____

____

____

____

____

____

Daily Page

Today I Traveled From: ______________________

To: ______________________

My Accommodation Today: ______________________

____

Best Food or Drink Today ______________________

____

Things I Did Today: ______________________

____

____

____

____

____

____

____

Souvenirs or Presents I Bought: ______________________

____

Quote or Phrase of the Day

____

____

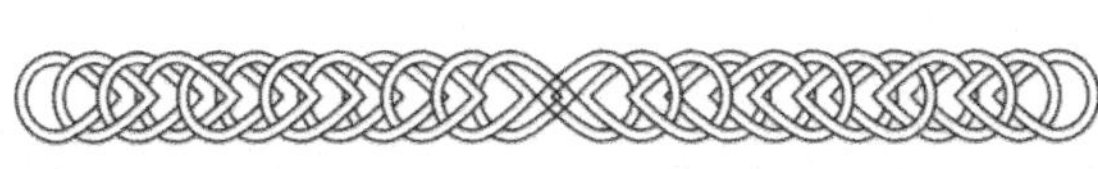

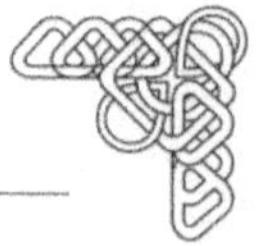

TODAY'S DATE : ____________________

What I'll Remember Most About Today…
--Experiences – Sights – Feelings--

Daily Page

Today I Traveled From: ______

To: ______

My Accommodation Today: ______

______

Best Food or Drink Today ______

______

Things I Did Today: ______

______

______

______

______

______

______

______

Souvenirs or Presents I Bought: ______

______

Quote or Phrase of the Day

______

______

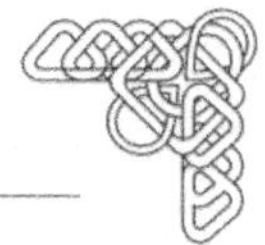

TODAY'S DATE : ______________________

What I'll Remember Most About Today…
--Experiences – Sights – Feelings--

Daily Page

Today I Traveled From: ______

To: ______

My Accommodation Today: ______

Best Food or Drink Today ______

Things I Did Today: ______

Souvenirs or Presents I Bought: ______

Quote or Phrase of the Day

TODAY'S DATE : ______________________

What I'll Remember Most About Today…
--Experiences – Sights – Feelings--

Daily Page

Today I Traveled From: ______

To: ______

My Accommodation Today: ______

______

Best Food or Drink Today ______

______

Things I Did Today: ______

______

______

______

______

______

______

______

Souvenirs or Presents I Bought: ______

______

Quote or Phrase of the Day

______

______

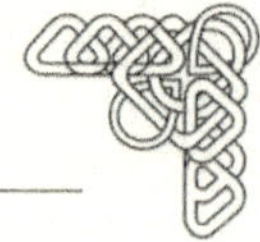

TODAY'S DATE : ____________________

What I'll Remember Most About Today…

--Experiences – Sights – Feelings--

____

____

____

____

____

____

g

Daily Page

Today I Traveled From: ______________________

To: ______________________

My Accommodation Today: ______________________

____

Best Food or Drink Today ______________________

____

Things I Did Today: ______________________

____

____

____

____

____

____

____

Souvenirs or Presents I Bought: ______________________

____

Quote or Phrase of the Day

____

____

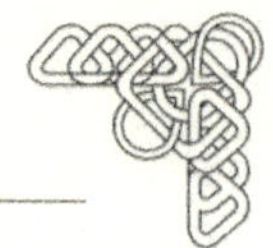

TODAY'S DATE : ______________________

What I'll Remember Most About Today…
--Experiences – Sights – Feelings--

____

____

____

____

____

____

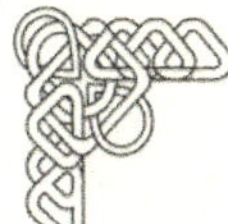
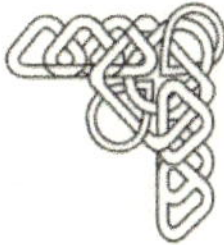

Daily Page

Today I Traveled From: ____________

To: ____________

My Accommodation Today: ____________

____

Best Food or Drink Today ____________

____

Things I Did Today: ____________

____

____

____

____

____

____

____

Souvenirs or Presents I Bought: ____________

____

Quote or Phrase of the Day

____

____

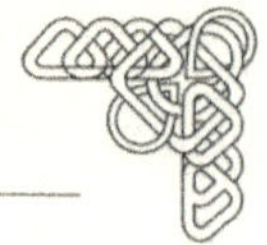

TODAY'S DATE : ___________________

What I'll Remember Most About Today…

--Experiences – Sights – Feelings--

Daily Page

Today I Traveled From: ______________________

To: ______________________

My Accommodation Today: ______________________

____

Best Food or Drink Today ______________________

____

Things I Did Today: ______________________

____

____

____

____

____

____

____

Souvenirs or Presents I Bought: ______________________

____

Quote or Phrase of the Day

____

____

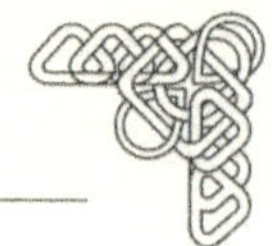

TODAY'S DATE : ______________________

What I'll Remember Most About Today…
--Experiences – Sights – Feelings--

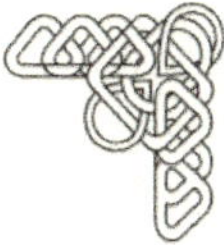

Daily Page

Today I Traveled From: ____________________

To: ____________________

My Accommodation Today: ____________________

Best Food or Drink Today ____________________

Things I Did Today: ____________________

Souvenirs or Presents I Bought: ____________________

Quote or Phrase of the Day

TODAY'S DATE : ______________________

What I'll Remember Most About Today...

--Experiences – Sights – Feelings--

____

____

____

____

____

____

Daily Page

Today I Traveled From: ______________________

To: ______________________

My Accommodation Today: ______________________

____

Best Food or Drink Today ______________________

____

Things I Did Today: ______________________

____

____

____

____

____

____

____

Souvenirs or Presents I Bought: ______________________

____

Quote or Phrase of the Day

____

____

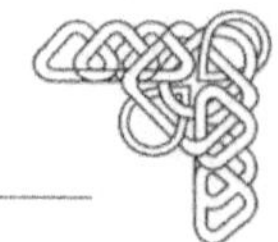

TODAY'S DATE : ____________________

What I'll Remember Most About Today...
--Experiences – Sights – Feelings--

Daily Page

Today I Traveled From: ______________________

To: ______________________

My Accommodation Today: ______________________

____

Best Food or Drink Today ______________________

____

Things I Did Today: ______________________

____

____

____

____

____

____

____

Souvenirs or Presents I Bought: ______________________

____

Quote or Phrase of the Day

____

____

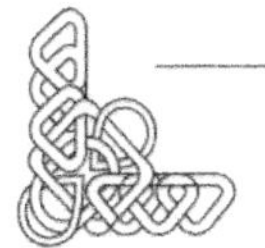

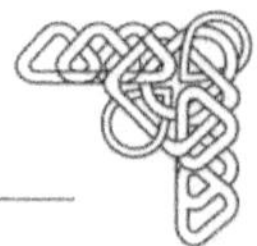

TODAY'S DATE : 

What I'll Remember Most About Today…
--Experiences – Sights – Feelings--

Daily Page

Today I Traveled From:

To:

My Accommodation Today:

Best Food or Drink Today

Things I Did Today:

Souvenirs or Presents I Bought:

Quote or Phrase of the Day

TODAY'S DATE : ____________________

What I'll Remember Most About Today…
--Experiences – Sights – Feelings--

Daily Page

Today I Traveled From: ______

To: ______

My Accommodation Today: ______

______

Best Food or Drink Today ______

______

Things I Did Today: ______

______

______

______

______

______

______

______

Souvenirs or Presents I Bought: ______

______

Quote or Phrase of the Day

______

______

TODAY'S DATE : ____________________

What I'll Remember Most About Today…
--Experiences – Sights – Feelings--

Daily Page

Today I Traveled From: ____________________

To: ____________________

My Accommodation Today: ____________________

____

Best Food or Drink Today ____________________

____

Things I Did Today: ____________________

____

____

____

____

____

____

____

Souvenirs or Presents I Bought: ____________________

____

Quote or Phrase of the Day

____

____

Record Of What I Spent During My Trip…

Daily Spending

Date :	

Accommodation :	Euro €	Dollars $
Transport :		
Food :		
Drink :		
Tickets/Admissions :		
Gifts :		
Misc :		
Today's Total :		

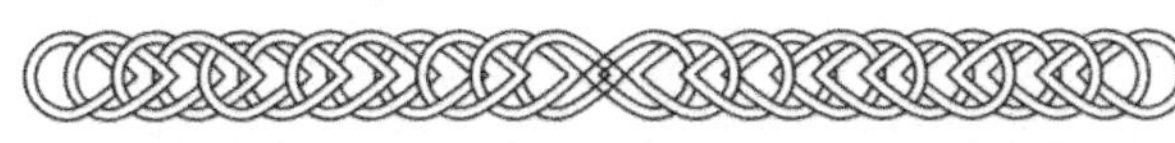

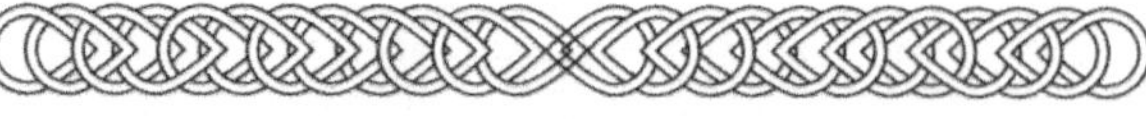

Daily Spending

Date :	

Accommodation :	Euro €	Dollars $
Transport :		
Food :		
Drink :		
Tickets/Admissions :		
Gifts :		
Misc :		
Today's Total :		

Daily Spending

Date :	

Accommodation :	Euro €	Dollars $
Transport :		
Food :		
Drink :		
Tickets/Admissions :		
Gifts :		
Misc :		
Today's Total :		

Daily Spending

Date :	

Accommodation :	Euro €	Dollars $
Transport :		
Food :		
Drink :		
Tickets/Admissions :		
Gifts :		
Misc :		
Today's Total :		

Daily Spending

Date :	

Accommodation :	Euro €	Dollars $
Transport :		
Food :		
Drink :		
Tickets/Admissions :		
Gifts :		
Misc :		
Today's Total :		

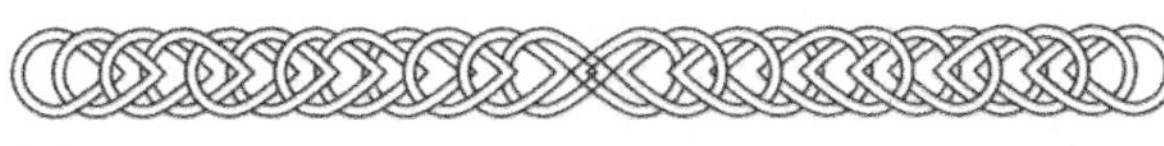

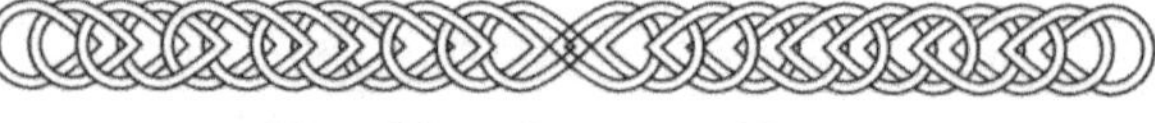

Daily Spending

Date :	

Accommodation :	Euro €	Dollars $
Transport :		
Food :		
Drink :		
Tickets/Admissions :		
Gifts :		
Misc :		
Today's Total :		

Daily Spending

Date :	

Accommodation :	Euro €	Dollars $
Transport :		
Food :		
Drink :		
Tickets/Admissions :		
Gifts :		
Misc :		
Today's Total :		

Daily Spending

Date :	

Accommodation :	Euro €	Dollars $
Transport :		
Food :		
Drink :		
Tickets/Admissions :		
Gifts :		
Misc :		
Today's Total :		

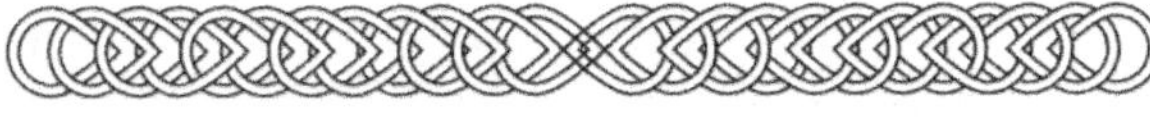

Daily Spending

Date :	

Accommodation :	Euro €	Dollars $
Transport :		
Food :		
Drink :		
Tickets/Admissions :		
Gifts :		
Misc :		
Today's Total :		

Daily Spending

Date :	

Accommodation :	Euro €	Dollars $
Transport :		
Food :		
Drink :		
Tickets/Admissions :		
Gifts :		
Misc :		
Today's Total :		

Daily Spending

Date :	

Accommodation :	Euro €	Dollars $
Transport :		
Food :		
Drink :		
Tickets/Admissions :		
Gifts :		
Misc :		
Today's Total :		

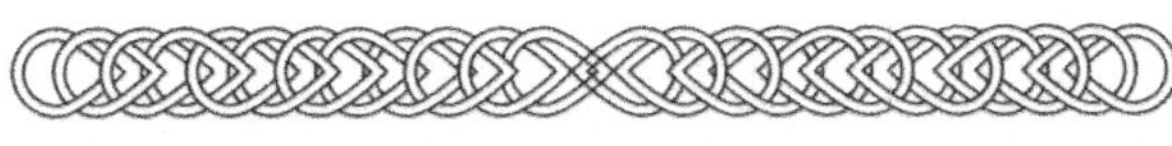

Daily Spending

Date :	

Accommodation :	Euro €	Dollars $
Transport :		
Food :		
Drink :		
Tickets/Admissions :		
Gifts :		
Misc :		
Today's Total :		

Daily Spending

Date :	

Accommodation :	Euro €	Dollars $
Transport :		
Food :		
Drink :		
Tickets/Admissions :		
Gifts :		
Misc :		
Today's Total :		

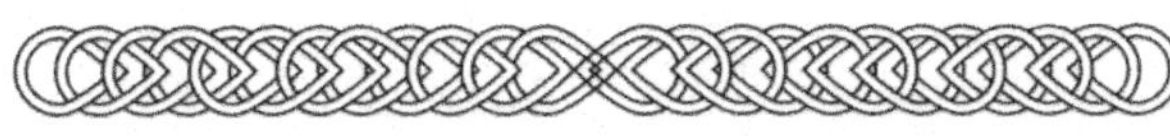

Daily Spending

Date :	

Accommodation :	Euro €	Dollars $
Transport :		
Food :		
Drink :		
Tickets/Admissions :		
Gifts :		
Misc :		
Today's Total :		

Daily Spending

Date :	

Accommodation :	Euro €	Dollars $
Transport :		
Food :		
Drink :		
Tickets/Admissions :		
Gifts :		
Misc :		
Today's Total :		

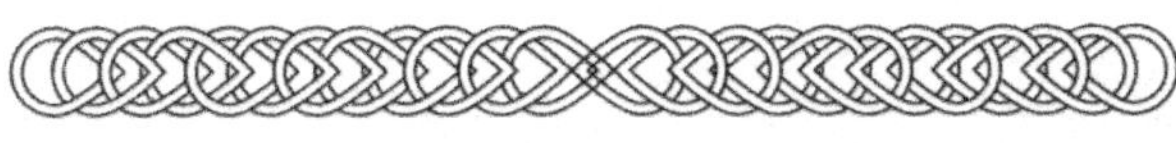

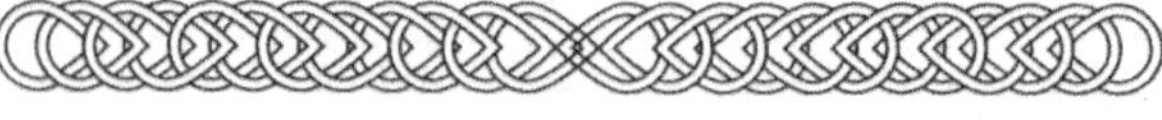

Daily Spending

Date :	

Accommodation :	Euro €	Dollars $
Transport :		
Food :		
Drink :		
Tickets/Admissions :		
Gifts :		
Misc :		
Today's Total :		

Daily Spending

Date :	

Accommodation :	Euro €	Dollars $
Transport :		
Food :		
Drink :		
Tickets/Admissions :		
Gifts :		
Misc :		
Today's Total :		

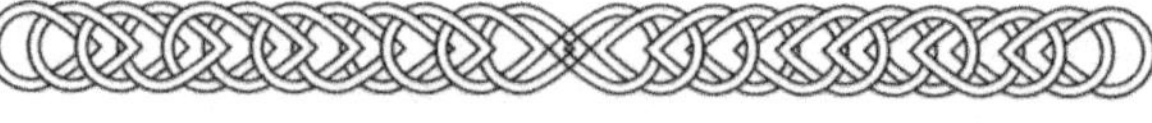

Daily Spending

Date :	

Accommodation :	Euro €	Dollars $
Transport :		
Food :		
Drink :		
Tickets/Admissions :		
Gifts :		
Misc :		
Today's Total :		

Daily Spending

Date :	

Accommodation :	Euro €	Dollars $
Transport :		
Food :		
Drink :		
Tickets/Admissions :		
Gifts :		
Misc :		
Today's Total :		

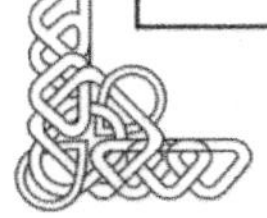
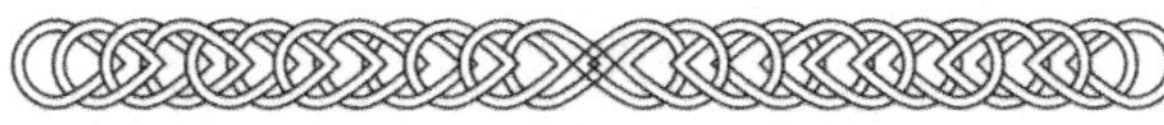

Daily Spending

Date :	

Accommodation :	Euro €	Dollars $
Transport :		
Food :		
Drink :		
Tickets/Admissions :		
Gifts :		
Misc :		
Today's Total :		

Daily Spending

Date :	

Accommodation :	Euro €	Dollars $
Transport :		
Food :		
Drink :		
Tickets/Admissions :		
Gifts :		
Misc :		
Today's Total :		

Daily Spending

Date :	

Accommodation :	Euro €	Dollars $
Transport :		
Food :		
Drink :		
Tickets/Admissions :		
Gifts :		
Misc :		
Today's Total :		

Daily Spending

Date :	

Accommodation :	Euro €	Dollars $
Transport :		
Food :		
Drink :		
Tickets/Admissions :		
Gifts :		
Misc :		
Today's Total :		

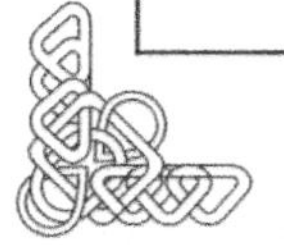

Daily Spending

Date :	

Accommodation :	Euro €	Dollars $
Transport :		
Food :		
Drink :		
Tickets/Admissions :		
Gifts :		
Misc :		
Today's Total :		

g

Daily Spending

Date :	

Accommodation :	Euro €	Dollars $
Transport :		
Food :		
Drink :		
Tickets/Admissions :		
Gifts :		
Misc :		
Today's Total :		

Daily Spending

Date :	

Accommodation :	Euro €	Dollars $
Transport :		
Food :		
Drink :		
Tickets/Admissions :		
Gifts :		
Misc :		
Today's Total :		

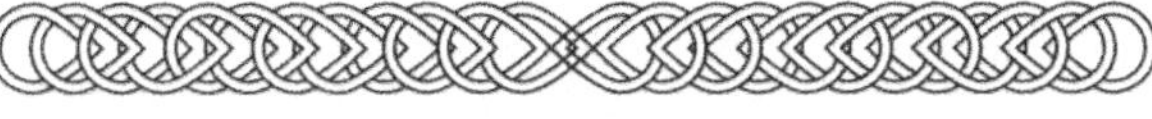

Daily Spending

Date :	

Accommodation :	Euro €	Dollars $
Transport :		
Food :		
Drink :		
Tickets/Admissions :		
Gifts :		
Misc :		
Today's Total :		

Daily Spending

Date :	

Accommodation :	Euro €	Dollars $
Transport :		
Food :		
Drink :		
Tickets/Admissions :		
Gifts :		
Misc :		
Today's Total :		

Daily Spending

Date :	

Accommodation :	Euro €	Dollars $
Transport :		
Food :		
Drink :		
Tickets/Admissions :		
Gifts :		
Misc :		
Today's Total :		

Great People I Met On My Trip To Ireland

Name :

Email :

Tel :

How We Met :

Notes :

Name :

Email :

Tel :

How We Met :

Notes :

Name :

Email :

Tel :

How We Met :

Notes :

Great People I Met On My Trip To Ireland

Name :

Email :

Tel :

How We Met :

Notes :

Name :

Email :

Tel :

How We Met :

Notes :

Name :

Email :

Tel :

How We Met :

Notes :

Great People I Met On My Trip To Ireland

Name :

Email :

Tel :

How We Met :

Notes :

Name :

Email :

Tel :

How We Met :

Notes :

Name :

Email :

Tel :

How We Met :

Notes :

Great People I Met On My Trip To Ireland

Name :

Email :

Tel :

How We Met :

Notes :

Name :

Email :

Tel :

How We Met :

Notes :

Name :

Email :

Tel :

How We Met :

Notes :

Notes For My Next Trip to Ireland

g

Could You Help Me?

DID YOU ENJOY THIS BOOK?
IF SO, YOU CAN MAKE A REAL DIFFERENCE!

Reviews are the most powerful tool when it comes to getting the word out about my books. I would love to be able to promote a book like the big publishing houses, but I'm just a one-man operation and can't take out full-page ads in the newspapers like they do. However, I do have a treasured resource that these publishers would do anything to get their hands on:

A kind and loyal group of readers who aren't afraid to share the love…

Sincere, honest reviews that come from the heart bring my books to the attention of other readers, who will hopefully enjoy them just as much.

If this book brought you a few moments of pleasure, I'd be forever grateful if you took a few minutes out of your busy day to leave a review (even just a couple of words would be appreciated) on the book's Amazon page.

You can get to the review page simply by scanning the QR code below.

Thanks! (Go raibh maith agat)

Look for other books from Mullarkey's Books of Ireland

...THERE'S LOTS MORE TO COME...

Disclaimer

ANOTHER BOOK YOU MAY ENJOY FROM MULLARKEY'S BOOKS OF IRELAND…

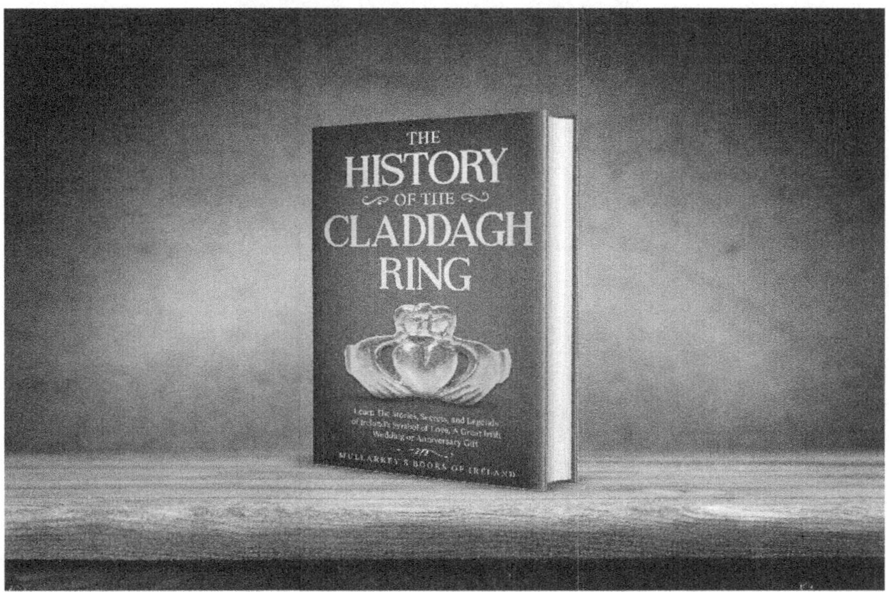

--Do you love Claddagh rings?
--Do you love all things Irish?

THEN, this little book is exactly right for you…

- Discover the fascinating history of the Claddagh ring
- Learn the legends associated with this symbol of Ireland

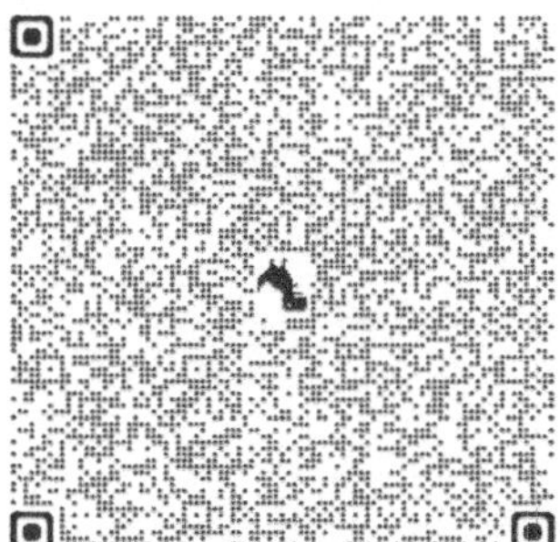

ANOTHER BOOK YOU MAY ENJOY FROM MULLARKEY'S BOOKS OF IRELAND...

DO YOU ABSOLUTELY LOVE CATS??
Did you know they played a huge role in Irish history? Like to know more...?
This funny, informative book tells you EVERYTHING you might possibly like to know about how cats shaped Irish history and culture...

STICKERS AND TICKETS

STICKERS AND TICKETS

STICKERS AND TICKETS

STICKERS AND TICKETS

STICKERS AND TICKETS

STICKERS AND TICKETS

STICKERS AND TICKETS

NOTES

NOTES

NOTES

NOTES

NOTES

NOTES

NOTES

NOTES

NOTES

NOTES

NOTES

NOTES
NOTES

Made in United States
North Haven, CT
09 June 2024